The Art of Teaching-
Way of the Warrior-teacher

The Art of Teaching–
Way of the Warrior–Teacher

Seth Austin Blevans

This edition published by Lulu Press.

2009 Lulu Press

ISBN 978-0-557-06419-9

Printed and bound in the United States of America

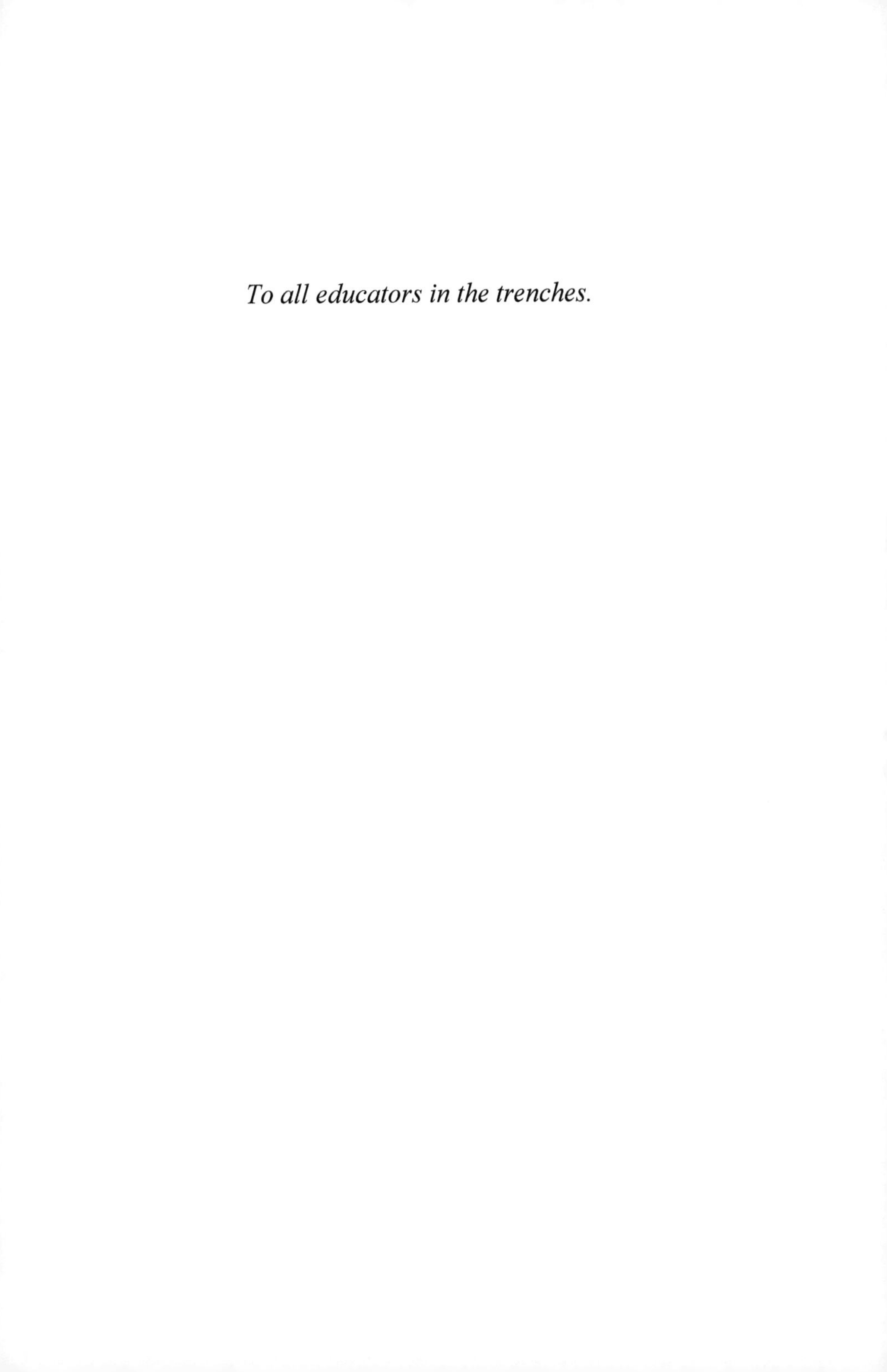

To all educators in the trenches.

Acknowledgments

Special thanks must go to Ralph D. Sawyer and the late Lionel Giles, for their excellent translations of Sun Tzu's Art of War. Without their expertise I would never have benefited from Sun Tzu's teachings.

I would like to recognize and thank all my friends who took time to give me feedback on this work. Extreme gratitude must go to: Allen Moore, for his invaluable computer assistance. Lastly, but never least, my wife, Kathleen, for her unwavering ability to be supportive, my first teacher (my mother, Beth) and my sons, Indigo, Caelin, Torin, Kieran, and Rafe for being in my life and making me a better teacher.

Teaching is a learning process. I am as much a product of good teaching experiences as bad. For each good teacher I had, I was taught by five burned-out, poor ones. Thank you to my students, all of my teachers (those who saw in me more than I did and those who let me fall through the, cracks.) and my coworkers (the good, the bad, the over-worked and the under paid). For without each and every one of their influences, I could not be the warrior that I am.

Contents

INTRODUCTION 12

1. STRATEGIC PLANNING 15
2. TENANTS OF EXPENSES 19
3. STRATAGEMISM OF DISCIPLINE 22
4. TACTICAL THINKING 27
5. STRUGGLING WITH ENERGY 31
6. BEING ADAPTIVE 35
7. MANEUVERING 39
8. TRAIL BLAZING 43

INTRODUCTION

The Art of Teaching was written for the reflective educator who strives for a deeper understanding of what it means to be a fighter for children and who looks deeper into the 'why' and 'how' students behave and act. The Art of Teaching is a book on strategy in and out of the classroom that is base on a 2400 year old book, The Art of War, by Sun Tzu. Much of Sun Tzu's work has been paraphrased and modified to speak to educators.

The wisdom of this ancient Chinese warrior-philosopher surpasses the context of war; it instructs a warrior on the importance of strategic thinking both on the battlefield and off. Over the centuries his teachings have been adopted as a paradigm for many business practices; from insights into human behavior to the closing of business transactions. What better form of modern warfare than that of business and its effects on social change during the 20th and 21st Century? There is an obvious natural progression from localized business-warfare to world social-economic and cultural warfare. The Art of Teaching offers strategic ways of seeing and acting during any type conflict; from dealing with large campaigns of school reform to the ability to deal with the psychological and interpersonal communication skills with students, parents, administrators, and peers.

Teaching is increasingly becoming a combative profession where legal and political skills must be united with the everyday aspects of teaching. The illusion of just teaching a specific subject falls away once one steps into a public classroom. The questions of; "What is the purpose of teaching?" and "What is the purpose of learning?" are of significant importance when one faces student apathy and open hostility toward learning. To teach one must have learned. To wage war one must have been in war. Thus education and warfare are linked by the common denominator of having experience and the ability to utilize that knowledge; this is the way of the Warrior-teacher.

Knowledge is not itself power. The application of knowledge offers one the tools to become powerful. It is in this light that this book is written. One must look to the ancient past to see how it will help us in the present. The teachings of Sun-Tzu are only words on paper until we transfer them into a cohesive pattern of action in our modern day classrooms.

Teaching children is an art form. Natural skill, deep conviction of moral and ethical responsibility, love of subject discipline, and passion to share what one knows with others are only a step toward the Art of Teaching. One must apply what is useful while discarding that which is deemed useless. One must then practice what is useful until one masters it. Only then can one be truly powerful. The value of what was written by Sun Tzu crosses cultural barriers and time. The genius of Sun Tzu was in his ability to see the patterns that govern human interaction on and off the battlefield. We humans are governed by the need to control others, thus we are governable by the same 'laws' that we impose on others. Our perception is limited by our understanding of our own reality. Sun Tzu was ruthless in dealing with the "enemy" but by his own teachings; he loved his enemy because he knew that hating an enemy only brought more hate. Only through loving those that must be dealt with, can one work toward a greater good. We must plan and then take decisive action by engaging the hearts and minds of our students with the love of the unknown so that we can teach them what we love and value. Is teaching children warfare? From the trenches of inner-city schools; where poverty is weighed by material items not knowledge, and where deep seated racial and social-economic anger coalesces with moral and ethical empathy to the wealthiest of suburbs, the answer is, "Yes!" We are fighting for those who do not have voices. We are fighting for those that do not know they have opportunities. We must battle the entrenched systems that hinder student learning and foster apathy for the under-represented. We are fighting to be better prepared in the classroom. We defend and protect the profession of education. We do all this and still we must protect and defend ourselves from physical, political, legal and economic attacks. Every educator must become more than a teacher; we must become warriors.

CHAPTER I
STRATEGIC PLANNING

"Goals dictate strategy. Strategy dictates tactics. Tactics dictate techniques. Techniques dictate results." A Warrior-teacher must be a strategist. When you begin to plan, you learn more about how and what is needed for your students to succeed. To reach your goal, you must have clear and measurable tasks. Always plan your course of action by knowing your audience. Know how your students think and you will be several steps ahead and better prepared to address any and all situations that might arise. The Warrior-teacher knows that teaching through strategy is vital to our society.

1. Educators determine what are the proper civil responsibilities by what we teach and how we teach. Remember the adage, "What is of importance must be monitored."

2. It is a matter of success or failure of our society, our

culture, our schools and our students that when you do not plan for the future, you are planning for failure. Thus, the Warrior-teacher must look toward what will benefit his students in life, not just meet an abstracted form of district and State evaluation.

3. One must learn to master one's perceptions of the people, places and conditions that influence a class. This practice becomes less daunting when the Warrior-teacher understands the four constant factors:

- Trust- "Respect is a two way street." Trust is the gift that a student gives when the Warrior-teacher has demonstrated mastery of the subject area, concern for the student and self-confidence in ability. Trust is the balance between the Warrior-teacher and the student. Students will bend over backwards for a Warrior-teacher whom they believe has earned their respect.

- Timing- "There is a time for all things." The Warrior-teacher knows that the time of day, duration of the periods and lessons, weather, and the seasons all affect the receptiveness of students.

- Environment- "All dangers great and small." Students go through a barrage of situations before they come to your classroom; late buses, interpersonal problems, lack of food, lack of sleep etc. An open mind and a sensible knowledge that students, be they children or young adults, are human beings who must be taught how to deal with the problems of everyday life while still being able to function in your room. One must have the strength of character to display 'benefit of doubt.' A Warrior-teacher must remember that children are not obligated to disclose any information about their personal lives and feelings, but you are responsible to help them find constructive ways to manage their emotions.

Command- "To lead, one must have been lead." Command is defined by the cardinal virtues of wisdom, sincerity, benevolence, courage and discipline. Wisdom is the knowledge of your own philosophy of teaching, of being a human being, living a life full of rich experiences, and educational curiosity that expands upon one's original education. A Warrior-teacher must have sincerity; the honesty and integrity in dealing with people, situations and most importantly oneself. A Warrior-teacher must show benevolence; the knowledge that students must not be held to the same strict standards as of an adult. A Warrior-teacher must have courage; the ability to fight for what one believes even though others do not hold the same convictions. Finally, a Warrior-teacher must be disciplined; one must have self-control and develop an ordered mind and practice.

4. Methods and forms of discipline dictate our ability to teach. Simply, one will not be able to teach a subject area until one has put into practice set procedures and routines. Rules must be set forth with their corresponding consequences. There must be consistancy when establishing a rule and following its appropriate consequence. When a Warrior-teacher disregards his own rules or deviates from the established consequences, that Warrior-teacher has lost credibility with all his students.

5. Reflect upon your practice. Question yourself on the condition of your classroom; "Are you trusted?" "Are you aware

of the advantages and disadvantages of time and environment?" "Are you consistent within your command?"

6. Profit from counsel, avail yourself of any helpful circumstances that might modify one's plans for the better. Be open to change but not for the sake of change. Consider your colleagues as wellsprings; some are fresh while others are all dried-up and a few may well be poisonous!

7. Do not be guided by abstract principles but by practical, measurable constructs that allow for energetic learning and teaching. The Warrior-teacher is dedicated to learning, but spends little effort on the revolving 'wheel of innovation.'

8. All education is based on deception. What seems easy could be difficult, what seems difficult could be easy! Never let your students become stagnant in your room. Throw them the curve balls that cause cognitive dissidence. Use bait to entice while also using feints to cause interest. The Warrior-teacher knows that deception and appropriate distraction are the heart of success or failure during student engagement.

CHAPTER 2

TENANTS OF EXPENSES

What is the inevitable cost on the minds, bodies and spirits of passionate Warrior-teachers? There are variables and a high price in waging battle in the classroom. Warrior-teachers, be forewarned, that to survive is not enough; one must thrive and grow stronger! These are the costs to grow stronger:

1. In all operations, there are expenses. He who wishes to teach must first tally the cost. The choice between helping your students and forgoing an extra luxury at home seems simple; but over time one will become emotionally attached to the purchases made with one's own money and demand greater acknowledgment and appreciation from students. This does one no good, for it will build resentment and eventually tear down the entire good work originally devised. Spend wisely and give

freely without any expectation of gratitude.

2. To undertake an endeavor, one must have the necessary supplies. There are consequences for all actions. Even the best course might bring with it a high price.

3. When you devise your goals, do not extend due dates unnecessarily. Interest will dull and focus will be strained. Be consistent in establishing and maintaining a time frame.

4. What can be accomplished quickly; do. What will take longer but is not difficult, finish early. What is of most importance and difficult must be done first.

5. Ration your supplies. What was once given freely might not be there the next time; take what is needed and store the remainder for future hard times. During difficult times one is most susceptible and thus this is the time you must work harder, more carefully and with less.

6. Ill-considered haste is better than ingenious but delayed operations. Speed may sometimes be injudicious; tardiness can never be anything but foolish- if only because it means impoverishment to the reputation of the Warrior-teacher. Spend your time planning but leave equal time for attending to other business. There must be balance in all things!

7. Flow from one topic to another; linking all together into a seamless unit of study. Take small steps back once in a while to allow review and rest before surging forward with renewed force.

8. The poverty of a school's or district's budget does not give free range to further impoverish the parents/guardians of one's students through requiring much needed materials. In many

cases money seems to solve most of a school's problems, but if the problem does not have anything to do with money; then one is throwing money away! Clearly establish the problem(s) before assessing a dollar figure.

9. Rewarding your students is necessary. Rewards must be a combination of intrinsic and extrinsic accolades. Praise for the sake of praise, ultimately gains one a negative result. One must present student work in a way that highlights it as a triumph. Reward group accomplishments in public while individual achievements should be recognized in a personal manner. This alleviates possible jealousy in the latter while increasing positive peer pressure in the former.

10. Everything changes. Striving for perfection of a single goal is the hallmark of all educational processes but it is far too narrow for the real world. Sometimes, what we learn to do is not applicable to everyday living. When goals or parameters change, so does everything else. The Warrior-teacher must adhere to this.

CHAPTER 3

STRATAGEMISM OF DISCIPLINE

"Discipline the behavior not the child." The Warrior-teacher knows that the child is separate from his/her behavior. Only those that are anti-social do not gravitate toward order. Do not dismiss nor resent those that have not or can not be taught in a normal structured environment. The Warrior-teacher knows that he must maintain a clear understanding that there must be set consequences for students' failure to follow rules while understanding that little can be done concerning the underlining reasons. This will alleviate the strain and emotional frustration over students' manipulation and/or anti-social behaviors.

1. In the practice of discipline, the primary goal is to mold the students' mind and influence the spirit. One must leave

the mind whole and intact; to shatter and destroy it is both morally and ethically reprehensible. It is far better to recapture a lost spirit or mind than to destroy it. Warrior-teachers do more than teach; they are role models. A Warrior-teacher must help to form the student through offering choices that expand their perspective of the world and how to interact with it.

2. To fight and conquer in all your dealings is not the ultimate goal. The ultimate goal is the manipulation of the student's resistance to learning without fighting. The Warrior-teacher knows that he must be fluid and wear away resistance at some points while wash away at others. There must be a pre-established channel that allows water to flow freely, otherwise there is a flood and then stagnation will follow.

3. The Warrior-teacher must be pro-active in all things. The highest strategic skill of a Warrior-teacher is the ability to foresee problems and neutralize them before they arise. Skillfully position yourself so that your focus is not on one group or a single student. Roam while keeping no specific pattern. Know where and how students travel so that you can narrow down access, slow movement, or direct flow to increase movement.

4. The worst form of discipline is to fully confront a child causing him/her to feel emotionally besieged. What is gained when one fights with a child? What are the types of points are earned when you get the final word or deal the ultimate punishment? The Warrior-teacher demonstrates sensitivity toward a child's feelings while prompting positive action and responsibility.

5. Overrunning a child's defenses will cost you much in the long run and the child little in the short run. What is at loss is

the Warrior-teacher's ability to have a positive impact upon the child while the child must only survive the initial attack and deal with the repercussions at a later time.

6. The Warrior-teacher subdues his students without fighting; he captures their will without laying siege, and neutralizes their ability to fight without lengthy operations. Give clear directions, time and opportunity to obey.

7. When your integrity is intact, you are free to dispute students' negative behavior and demonstrate true authority. This is the method of attacking by stratagem.

8. The rule of teaching is the same as the rule of war; a weapon cannot be blunted if it is not in use, but to keep its keenness one must unsheathe it. Control in the classroom is an illusion. The secret lies not in controlling students but in earning their respect. Respect is gained through honest actions, and clearly presented convictions; not through intimidation.

9. Emotions are neither right nor wrong. It is the student's actions that define right or wrong. The Warrior-teacher knows that his students' emotional state affects all encounters. Humans are social creatures that display rational and irrational behaviors according to unlimited variables The Warrior-teacher knows this and uses it to his advantage.

10. Let no slight of respect go unchecked. This does not mean that the slightest remark or action must be dealt with the harshest of treatment, but rather that each remark or action must be openly noticed and some type of corrective action must be given.

11. The Warrior-teacher is the bulwark of the school. If

the bulwark is competent in all areas, the school will be strong. If the bulwark is defective, the school will be weak.

12. When there is restlessness and distrustfulness in the ranks of students, trouble will come from the outside. Students are not stupid; they are self-serving, calculating, and manipulative creatures that will grow up into adults with long emotional memories. Thus, students will always find ways to make their lives easier while inflicting revenge when a self-justified opportunity is presented.

13. The Warrior-teacher knows and follows the five essential beliefs that lead to victories in all conflicts:

- He will win who knows when to fight and when not to fight. One must know when to take the offensive or the defensive in all actions.

- He will win who knows how to handle both physical and emotional conflicts.

- He will win when ones' students are engaged with the same spirit of success as the Warrior-teacher.

- He will win when he is both prepared and prepares his students.

- He will win who has an unwavering philosophy of purpose. Thus, self-knowledge coupled with knowledge of one's students will lead to victory in all things.

14. If you know your students and know yourself, you need not fear the result of any confrontation. If you know yourself but not your students, for every conflict resolved, you will also suffer a defeat. If you know neither the student nor yourself, you will succumb in every conflict.

CHAPTER 4
TACTICAL THINKING

"Know yourself, so that you will better know others, and to know others is to better know yourself." The Warrior-teacher secures success by modifying tactics when necessary. The power of self-knowledge and that of optimism are linked. If one knows what makes him/her happy or unhappy, there is power to dictate one's perspective for the better or worse. Action is both a physical and mental activity.

1. To be knowledgeable is to be aware of what is known and aware of the lack of knowledge of those around you.

2. Water is neither good nor bad. Its path varies due to resistance and abundance. To secure ourselves against failure lies in our own hands, but the opportunity to fail is also in our own hands.

3. The Warrior-teacher is able to secure himself against defeat by concealing his full motives and taking unremitting precautions through over-planning.

4. The Warrior-teacher sows for the future with the clear understanding that what is planted might not be viewed when grown.

5. Acclaim of excellence for a job well done, when it is a common job is not true excellence. True excellence should be considered both as specialized attributes and consistent commitment towards proper action. What is of importance is not the skillful student who can accomplish what he already knows but rather what those who do not know can accomplish after learning something new.

6. The Warrior-teacher is one who teaches with ease and excels without acclaim. He who only sees the obvious has students learning shallowly, he who looks deeper and sees the greater picture has students learning with depth.

7. The Warrior-teacher knows that success might not bring him reputation for wisdom or credit for his determination. The world at large might not know what he has accomplished; for the Warrior-teacher does not look toward heightened reputation.

8. The Warrior-teacher teaches by making no purposeful mistakes. Mistakes offer areas that need to be rectified but the cost can be wasted time and energy. The Warrior-teacher will look into the future and discern conditions that are not yet manifested and never make the same mistakes in the same way twice.

9. Look only toward success and one will win. Look

only toward failure and one will lose. One who plans for success succeeds, while one who does not plan plans for failure.

10. In all forms of planning, the Warrior-teacher must know and utilize the five areas of tactical thinking. Each area is linked to the other. Each area of knowledge must be considered united in purpose.

- The ability to survey and measure the lay of the land. This allows opportunities for success.

- The ability to perceive and know that each person has their own agenda. This allows for deeper understanding of others behaviors and actions.

- The ability to budget supplies, finances and to estimate all conditions that affects choices. One must be aware of what one values and plan accordingly.

- The ability to balance the risks and variables that each and every endeavor is defined by.

- The ability to define one's goals and separate the "wants" from the "needs."

- The ability to reach students through direct and indirect means. Direct means are concrete in nature and thus they are able to be evaluated. Indirect means are flexible in nature and bolster knowledge through non measurable avenues.

11. The Warrior-teacher knows that reality is often inconvenient. One has the choice to ignore what is not working or swallow one's pride and change.

12. Too often educators seem oblivious to the fact that they are under constant scrutinizing from students, peers, parents, administrators and the public.

13. Know that once something is written, it develops into a possible legal document that has the propensity to be used against you for as long as the document is floating around.

14. The truest form of teaching comes not from the observed tactics and techniques but by the end result. It is not important for students to understand either the tactics or the techniques that brought them success, but for them to be swept away by the outcome.

15. Students are not impressed by the tactics and techniques uses in the classroom; they remember the end result. It is through the outcome that love of learning is created. Later in the journey of education, interest in the tactics and techniques are developed.

16. The Warrior-teacher must be clear and concise in all written formats and verbal interactions. Lengthy discourse allows for misinterpretation or erroneous statements.

CHAPTER 5
STRUGGLING WITH ENERGY

What is the cost to your energies, your personal life, and your waist line? Do you have time to read for yourself? Do you have time to exercise or play? Do your children remember who you are? Too often teaching becomes more a balancing act between out of classroom requirements and teaching. The day-to-day struggles of extra duties, home life, and economics tax one's strength and focus. There must be greater importance placed on managing one's own energy which will, in turn, allow one to carry out more work over a greater length of time. Quite often one must struggle with the ebb and flow of energy, both from students and from one's self. Balancing all the varied and non-cohesive aspects of teaching takes a toll. There must be balance within and without your profession. How often do you stay late at work? How much personal and or family time is taken during grading, planning lessons, and volunteering?

The Warrior-teacher must balance his passion for teaching with varied personal passions in and out of the classroom. There might be many different areas at which one strives to excel but have you found the tricks to save time, energy and squeeze extra hours into your day? This is the Warrior-teacher's struggle with energy.

1. Managing a large class follows the same principles as managing a smaller one; it is merely a question of dividing up students into smaller groups. There is also a psychological aspect, where one is better able to work with perceived smaller numbers when students are in groups than working with one large mass. The Warrior-teacher sees the tree in a grove rather than missing the tree because it is hidden in the forest.

2. One must institute routines and procedures to successfully establish a cohesive classroom. Routines dictate the standards while procedures guide practice

3. The ability to grind away students' lack of interest and/or interests in extraneous things is based on developing ones' strengths and knowing your students. A strong personality outshines most distractions.

4. Your ability to manage a class through barrages of interruptions is based on effective maneuvering of direct and indirect approaches. In direct approaches, one may gain one's objective, but only through indirect methods can one secure one's goals. Direct approaches are the standard lectures while the hands-on, small tasks approach, falls under the indirect concept.

5. It is important to display self-restraint when teaching. Use of judgment will allow one to bring to bear what is necessary at the right time. One's inability to wait for a student's

comprehension will ultimately define the quality of the Warrior-teacher.

6. The Warrior-teacher will be forceful, and competent in the onset, and prompt in all decisions. A Warrior-teacher must be slow to make a promise, and quick to keep them.

7. Energy may be likened to the bending of a bow and decision to the release of an arrow. If one is complacent in an action the effect will be small. One must place the right amount of energy for the desired effect; too much energy and one is tapped, too little energy will be hazardous to the objective; all the while having the goal forefront in mind. Energy is expendable, thus it must be valued!

8. Amid any turmoil, your class will look toward you with confidence if there are pre-arranged and practiced signals. You must have a disciplined class if you are to direct movement. Security is in your hands.

9. To show true strength, one must display what is commonly considered weakness. To hide perceived weakness, one must convey strength.

10. The Warrior-teacher will motivate through all ways necessary to complete the objective.

11. The Warrior-teacher looks toward harvesting the positive energies of a class so that the negative energies burn away.

12. Consider the talents and capabilities of your students so that the talented help those less talented and those of least talent are not judged by the same standards. This is the use of natural and inherent energy within the classroom.

13. The outcome of a disciplined and highly trained Warrior-teacher to that of a demoralized and highly trained teacher is vastly different. Motivation is energy and energy is what fuels success in all things. Motivation is contagious in either positive or negative ways.

14. Conserve your energy; it is the nature of water to remain motionless without interference. Use student's energy to bolster your own supply. Delve into their excitement and become buoyant by the flood of their youth and exuberance.

15. The Warrior-teacher knows that energy will be influenced by other forms of energy. Excitement from a teacher will build students' excitement and interest; while lack of teacher excitement will further reduce student engagement.

16. Great results can be achieved with little.

CHAPTER 6
BEING ADAPTIVE

"Strength is developed by challenges, thus to be powerful one must be tested." Developing consistent and strict routines and procedures are intended to foster student achievement and alleviate misbehaviors. This does not mean that one's ability to be adaptive must atrophy. Water will always rise to find its own level, seek the path of least resistance, and bend when it meets a stronger entity. The Warrior-teacher knows this and becomes like water.

1. The Warrior-teacher who is prepared has time to observe the actions of students, but the Warrior-teacher who is late or neglectful in being prepared must hasten in all actions, risk missing opportunities and be forced to confront many more obstacles.

2. The Warrior-teacher imposes the standard of excellence and never allows the students to impose the level of

standard upon the teacher.

3. As in all battles, the Warrior-teacher knows that to hold the advantage one must:

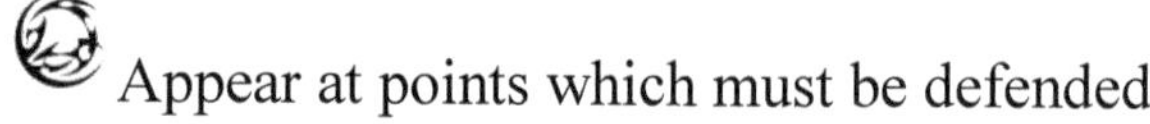

Appear at points which must be defended.

March swiftly to places that are not expected.

Emerge from the unseen and strike quickly and decisively.

Avoid places that are defended.

4. You can only defend what is observed as being weak. What are your weaknesses? What type of "buttons" can a student push that may cause you to lose control? Defend all places, even those that are not likely to be attacked. The Warrior-teacher knows the less likely an attack might come, the more likely that it will happen.

5. Through knowing the hearts and minds of one's students and finding no resistance, one may rest. But for any student who resist, haste must be made and many preparations made.

6. One must be aware of the timing, use, and dangers of "bluffs."

7. The use of 'divide and conquer' is effective if one keeps plans hidden.

8. To avoid disaster, it is better to protect from the

greatest not the minor. One risks a major disaster if all concentration is focused on protecting each tiny weakness. This is folly, for it will weaken the whole instead of protecting it; the minor will be dealt with in due course. Acquiesce in the small misfortune to avoid the great!

9. Show strength through self-confidence. For the greatest skill comes from compelling the enemy to disperse while simultaneously striking with greater force at the fractured areas.

10. Power is an illusion. What is perceived as our strengths, our sense of safety and resolve to act will be tried and fail at some point. It is the true Warrior-teacher that will rebuild and grow stronger through these trials.

11. Clarity of one's plans and insight into how one's students may disrupt those plans will allow for greater likelihood of success.

12. Rouse students to see what interests them or holds no interest. Force your students to reveal themselves so as to find the best way to reach them.

13. Carefully compare classes to see what works and what does not.

14. Do not simply repeat tactics because they worked before; rather let your methods be regulated by the circumstances and opportunities presented to you.

15. Everyone can see the superficiality of the perceived ability to teach. What is not seen is the long series of plans that have been built into the process of teaching the subject. The strands that are woven are strong and flexible but translucent.

16. Teaching is like the action of water; water will follow the path of least resistance and will always run swiftly down hill. Water shapes its course according to the nature of the land, thus the Warrior-teacher works toward his practice in relation to the student and the environment

17. In teaching, avoid what is learned and focus on what is weak.

18. When dealing with angry students, leave an opening for them to escape gracefully; this opening could be emotional or physical. Allow for tempers to lessen and regroup.

19. The Warrior-teacher who can modify his lessons in relationship to the student is a master Warrior-teacher.

CHAPTER 7
MANEUVERING

What type of school environment do you work in? What type of neighborhood do your students live in? What are the social economical background(s) of your students? These questions and others should lead you to an understanding of the terrain that one must traverse daily. Maneuvering is not travel but rather progression toward or away from what inevitably must be a common goal. If one is waging a struggle against failure, from falling test scores to attendance, the Warrior-teacher knows that maneuvering toward a common goal must be both a school-wide and an individual process, if true growth is to take place. Maneuvering also implies knowing your ground and history. The Warrior-teacher maneuvers around all obstacles and looks for the advantage in all things.

1. There must be a clear and practiced hierarchy of power. Leadership directs and defines responsibility of action. If one chooses to skip a level of authority, there is both a breakdown

of leadership and a stated lack of trust.

2. Once the common goal is agreed upon, the differences between skills and experience must be blended and harmonized into a cohesive group. There are experts for all facets of an endeavor. Use these experts to train others. Those with the least and/or fewest skills should be employed for their labor.

3. There are topics or situations that are too narrow to navigate safely. One invites attack in such situations. No situation that can not be legitimately defended should be considered as safe nor should any situation that has no value be considered as valid. It is a great mistake to waste energy and risk danger over unimportant goals when the same amount of energy and danger will lead to greater success.

4. There will be times that one will have to be circumspect so that others will be more inclined to help. Diplomacy will alleviate much misunderstanding while allowing for jaded personnel to become productive. The goal is to turn those who would inhibit into those who will become advocates. Move others around your goals. Know that each person has an agenda. To know that agenda, allows one to better understand the motivations and actions of a person. Once you know this, opportunities avail themselves.

5. Undertaking any endeavor will be hazardous if one's forces are not disciplined. One may be knowledgeable about the topic or situation, or know with certainly the 'lay of the land,' but fail to bring their knowledge to bear in practical matters. The Warrior-teacher displays versatility of mind to see the possibilities in any situation while also knowing all situations can lead to many types of various successes or uncountable forms of

failures.

6. Hurried and harassed endeavors will lead to exhaustion. Last minute does not mean top priority.

7. Do not focus solely on one type of success. Allow for success and failures. Small successes do not always manifest into victories. Small failures do not always lead to disaster.

8. Focus on the solution not the problem. One must learn to develop the type of mind that sees difficulties as opportunities and how to seize an advantage when extricating from misfortune.

9. Reduce hostilities by inflicting subtleties of action. The old adage of "work smarter not harder" must be taken to heart.

10. Be like water; forceful when necessary, while always polishing what is already there. Find ways to entice subvert and wear down your adversaries from their cause of action without causing you to lose energy or sense of self. One can quickly loose 'face' if one is not ethical or moral in word or deed. Always keep in mind that one's words and actions are an extension of one's own sense of self.

11. The Warrior-teacher knows that problems will arise at the most inopportune times. Always over-plan in all that is important.

12. The Warrior-teacher knows that there are five dangerous character faults:

Reckless behaviors that lead to blind and desperate actions. If one always "jumps before one looks" the consequences are rarely devastating.

Unwillingness to take risks will lead to certain failure. "What is not ventured is never gained!" Worse, one who openly makes preparations for failure destroys one's support for success.

Haste in anger due to ease of being provoked. One must have the emotional state of mind that is not devoid of logical reasoning and allows for humor to supercede anger.

Exaggerated sense of self-importance. One must be humble in regarding one's accomplishments, confident in one's ability and honest in one's failings.

Lack of empathy will destroy trust, respect and professional standing. One must have empathy without feeling obligated to solve, fix or mend others' problems. The Warrior-teacher knows that feelings of obligation often leads to resentful actions; act and give in an unconditional manner.

13. The Warrior-teacher knows that to punish transgressions before trust is established is to court subversive behaviors. If trust is established but transgressors are not punished for their offensives, there will be subversive behaviors. Thus, the Warrior-teacher commands with strict and consistent discipline.

CHAPTER 8
TRAIL BLAZING

"Blaze new trails while remembering the paths forged in past times." The needs of a Warrior-teacher must always derive from the needs of the students. Without students, there is no need for the Warrior-teacher. Thus, an educator must strive to find new ways to engage the minds and hearts of students. The Warrior-teacher knows that delving into any new territory, one must be aware of landmarks and danger signs.

1. Do not linger in foreign territory without prior knowledge of the lay of the land. Knowledge of your subject is not enough; one must know how to disseminate it.

2. Choose areas that have far reaching perspectives rather than narrow, shortsighted views. Broaden your student's perspectives. Youth is a lack of experience, not just lack of age.

3. After bridging a possibly dangerous topic, move on

quickly. If confronted, state the reason truthfully but always couch truth with reason.

4. Never hinder your student's learning with your own excitement to teach. Create an opening for your students to meet you and thus they will be receptive to your teaching.

5. Always be prepared by scouting out ahead of your students. Be further ahead than your students so that natural progression and flow of assigned tasks come easily rather than having to work 'up-stream.'

6. In dry, boring areas, bolster your students with what has been covered in the past, surround your students with what is to be covered in the present, and bring to the forefront what must be covered in the future.

7. Remember, all students prefer to know the lay of the land and be assured what is to follow.

8. Occupy the cheerful side of topics so that your students can benefit from the light but also present the reality and distinction of the dark side.

9. When a situation arises that risks to over-flow the banks of political, social or educational safety, wait for the river of danger to subside before you ford it.

10. Areas that hold natural dangers should be skirted quickly and not approached if at all possible. The Warrior-teacher knows that what is of interest to him might not be appropriate for his students.

11. When facing dangerous topics, one must be aware of insidious ears and be prepared for an ambush from friends and

foes. Do not assume innocent topics will be perceived or viewed as such by others.

12. When students or peers seem to provoke a conflict, beware of the alternative factors taking place. Students will find ways to distract you when they are bored or sense your lack of interest.

13. Sudden movement or noise in groups indicates problems/dangers that must be attended too. Whenever you are involved in areas of possible dangers, look for signs that point to trouble. Keep circulating around so as to be attentive to all students and situations.

14. When an angry student engages his/her friends to come to their assistance, this indicates a possible attack. This attack could be direct or indirect in nature. Direct attack lends itself to the verbal or physical arena; while an indirect attack leads to demoralization of the student body or to negative forms of gossip. The Warrior-teacher knows that indirect attacks are often the more dangerous in the long run.

15. Frivolous proposals of compromise are an indication of malfeasance. Do not give into the temptation of compromise. Choose what must be done for the greater good then for the immediate present.

16. The sign of whispering in small groups is a possible sign of dissatisfaction and loss of control.

17. Too frequent rewards or compliments are a sign of exhaustion and lack of trust of one's students or one's control of the students! Conversely, too many punishments or threats betray a lack of control; unwarranted forms of punishment points to loss

of discipline.

18. The action to threaten and then renege ruins discipline and trust. To reward those who have been threatened causes resentment and lack of respect from other students.

19. When a student offers an apology, accept the apology and move on to negotiations. Never allow disrespect to be viewed as acceptable behavior. Always address it and make time to resolve the situation

20. Do not dismiss the small, the young, or the female student as a small threat. A Warrior-teacher who does not exercise good judgment is sure to be caught unawares.

21. The truth of maintaining disciple is that a Warrior-teacher must gain the students' trust before true discipline can be established. A road must be made and traveled upon to gain trust. With true discipline, students will learn and follow directions; otherwise a Warrior-teacher can not do his job.

22. There are six tenants to creating order before students can be taught:

- When seeking to educate, the mind must be enticed before taught. True discipline establishes quiet within the storm of student egotism.

- When a Warrior-teacher has confidence, his students will follow his directions. Otherwise, students will seek re-assurance during each step of the way.

- When a teacher is weak in discipline, his students will

subvert his power. When a teacher is too strict in discipline there will be a collapse in his authority.

When students are faced with overwhelming odds without being properly prepared, the result will be emotional distress, lack of productivity and ultimately failure in desired objectives.

When teachers are faced with leaders that demonstrate a collapse in authority, there will be ruin within the school.

When principal's or district's directions or mandates are unclear or confusing, the perception is that they have demonstrated weak authority, and the end result is utter disorganization.

23. The Warrior-teacher is only as good as his ability and his commitment to his practice.

www.ingramcontent.com/pod-product-compliance
Ingram Content Group UK Ltd.
Pitfield, Milton Keynes, MK11 3LW, UK
UKHW020230250726
13967UKWH00001B/284

9 780557 064199